Eamonn O'
Christine

GW01003310

# THE ART OF STILLNESS
## Meditation and Relaxation
## in the Christian Life

*VERITAS*

Published 1997 by
Veritas Publications
7-8 Lower Abbey Street
Dublin 1

Copyright © Eamonn O'Gorman & Christine Kelly 1997

ISBN 1 85390 307 8

British Library Cataloguing
in Publication Data.
A catalogue record for
this book is available
from the British Library.

Cover design: Lucia Happel
Illustrations: Charles Shore
Printed in the Republic of Ireland by Betaprint Ltd, Dublin

# Contents

# Introduction

The reason why we have chosen to produce this work is that we believe that 'meditation' is, or at least should be, an integral part of Christian development in the educational process. We have been involved in this work for the last fifteen years and we have enjoyed this opportunity to put on paper, in an ordered fashion, some of the work which we have undertaken in this regard.

Over these years we have noticed a growing antipathy among students to 'imposed religion'. Upon reflection we wished to approach this problem from another angle, and we hoped to counteract their indifference with an awakening desire to know God on a personal basis.

We have found that scripturally-based meditation, combined with a sound holistic emphasis, meets this need admirably. Many young people in today's world suffer from low self-esteem. Meditation confirms them in their own self-worth, thus opening and making them receptive to the power of the Spirit who dwells within them. We have been agreeably surprised and gratified by the positive feedback, and by their ability to integrate into their experience such concepts as awareness, silence, focusing, being etc.

The exercises and meditations which follow are those which we have used very successfully in class.

# Preface

Dear Reader,

Our purpose in writing the following meditations is to reach you, the reader and meditator, where you are at. In so doing, we would like you to experience who you are, and grow into an awareness of your inner depths.

In using the meditations in this book it is hoped that you would come to an experience of God, as your Father, as Jesus your friend, brother, and companion who is one with the Father and therefore can bring you to full knowledge of him, as the Holy Spirit who is the power of love in your life, a free gift given to you in Jesus.

When we come to know ourselves, we then have the basis, a starting-point to communicate with the Lord and to build a relationship with him.

Like any relationship it takes time. To come to know the Lord we need to spend time with him. To come to know ourselves we need time … to listen… to our dreams and, our hopes and to know our inner thoughts. When we learn to 'spend time' we have something to bring into a relationship, we can start to relate and share.

These meditations can be used either in a group setting … or on your own in the quietness of your room. Their duration can be five minutes to one hour, the time span is up to you.

These meditations are appropriate for all age groups, but in a special way they speak to anyone who is searching and journeying on a pilgrimage of faith. At the same time they are broad enough not to encroach on anyone's freedom. Most of us are searching for an understanding of ourselves, and the mysteries of life.

These meditations are meant as a form of nurturing; they

will feed a desire and give you a glimpse of the mystical life that belongs to each person by the mere fact of their 'being'... conceived in the the heart of God-given life through Jesus and graced by the Holy Spirit. I hope they will bring you into an awareness of what is already yours.

The mysteries of the Love of God are endless. Therefore, for each one it is the adventure of a life time! What God waits to reveal to those who grow in love for him is beyond immagination.

For each one there is your own 'inner room', the 'centre' of your creation where God lives.... in time. With practice it will be possible to close your eyes and enter your inner room where you can commune with your God.

It is, however, important to find a quiet place, create an atmosphere conducive to meditation and do some awareness exercises, to, as it were, tune yourself in. It is important to remember that meditation is time for 'YOU' to 'BE' – to remain empty, without thought.

The six-week course beginning on p. 78 has been used with secondary school and adult groups. These meditations are only guidelines and are flexible, leaving space for you to change as inspiration leads you.

We hope these meditations will aid you in your search. The blessings of God are already yours. May you grow in awareness... and be filled with the fruits of love.

We would like to thank Veritas for their commitment to publishing this book and tape and Michael Kelleher for his assistence with the illustrations.

# Preparation exercises before meditation

For anything that is new, any new interest or hobby, some preparation is always needed. Meditation, for those of us whose minds and hearing are used to the noise level of a disco, the television, or a personal stereo... needs not a warming up period, but rather a cooling or winding down period. Here are a few exercises we would recommend as a preparation preceding the meditation.

Most of us are aware of the things around us, but how conscious are we of our bodies, and the daily functions we take for granted? So before we attempt to journey inward let us do these exercises that make us aware of ourselves and our bodies.

One small piece of advice: take your time. The exercises are not meant to be gone through quickly. Allow what you read and/or hear to take its time and course in the places of relaxation.

# 1. Awareness

1. First become conscious of how you are sitting now... are you upright?... or slumped?... are your legs crossed?... is your chin resting on your hand?... Just become aware of how you are sitting now... become aware of the different textures in your skin; if, for example, your chin is resting on your hand... become aware of the material on your legs. What do your socks, tights, trousers or skirt, feel like as they touch your skin? Maybe this is something you haven't been aware of before.

2. For our second exercise I would like you to wiggle your toes, become conscious of how they feel when you move them, how each toe feels individual yet a part of your foot. Do the same

with your fingers... now spread your fingers and feel the air flow between each finger... these exercises may seem silly but you are becoming aware.

3. For the third exercise I want you to close your eyes... now open them... I want you to do this again but become aware of your eyelids as they close. What sensation do you feel? Then open them. Do this a couple of times slowly, being aware of what you sense and how you feel.

4. Become aware of the air that you breathe in, just breathe normally, but you become aware that the air you... breathe in... is cold... and the air you... breathe out... is warm. Lets try this once more... breathe in...
Now take a... DEEP breath in... you will feel the cold air enter through your nostrils and your lungs expand...
Breathe out slowly... you will feel the warm air through your nostrils as your lungs collapse... Let's try this once more.

Now that you have become a little more aware of your bodies, you may enter the discovery of meditation and your inner selves.

# 2. Breathing

Begin by exaggerating your breathing to help you become aware of your breath... breathe in deeply.... pause and breathe out... be aware of how your lungs expand, on your inward breath, and your stomach fills with air, and on exhaling, both your lungs and stomach collapse... Repeat ... breathe in... Pause... breathe out... Again breathe in... Pause... breathe out...

Empty all thought from your mind and concentrate on the 'filling' and the 'emptying'. Filling with life and emptying the negative... breathe in deeply... pause... and breathe out... Repeat... Empty all thought, be aware of your body filling and emptying ...

Now, as you breathe, this time be aware of the cold air that enters through your nose and the warm air that leaves. Breathe in deeply... pause and breathe out... Just concentrate on the cold air entering your nostrils and the warm air leaving ...Think of nothing else... the cold air entering and the warm air leaving ... Repeat ... breathe in deeply... pause and breathe out...

As you breathe in this time, you are aware of life that enters, and on breathing out, you experience freedom. You are breathing out anything that you don't need for life.
Breathe in life ...pause ... breathe out, releasing anything that hinders you from living ... Now relax ... Breathe in life ...pause ... breathe out, release anything that hinders you from living ... Relax... Allow this life to enter the very depth of your being ... Again... breathe in ... pause ... breathe out ...

# 3. Body Awareness

Become aware of your body and the contact between your body and the surface of the floor or chair.

Breathe deeply and relax.

Start with your head... slowly move your head in circular motion from right to left and relax... Now do the same movement from left to right... and relax...

Now raise your head from the ground to your chest... hold for a count of two and relax... Repeat... If you are sitting bend your head so that your chin comes into contact with your chest.

Now to your right shoulder... move it up and around in a circular movement and relax ... Repeat... Now your left shoulder... moving it up, and around in a circular movement and relax... repeat ...
Your stomach muscles, pull them in tightly, hold, and relax... Repeat...

Raise your right arm about two inches... hold... feel its weight... the pull of the muscles... and slowly lower your arm and relax. Now your left arm... Repeat ...

Clench your fists and tighten the muscles in both your arms ... hold it ... and relax ...

Push your heels out and bring your toes towards you, hold... relax ...
Now gently tighten the calf and thigh muscles... Relax

Stretch all the muscles of your body, as you would when you first wake up in the morning, stretch, and relax...

Open your mouth as wide as you can, feel the pull and tension, be aware of the blood flow through your lips.... Relax

Now for your eyes; open your eyes as widely as you can, be aware of the raising of your eyebrows, the tightness at the corner of your eye sockets... close your eyes... be aware that your eyelids are like shutters that open and close to allow light

in, and to shut the light out... do this exercise once again ...
open these shutters and be aware of the moist inner eye that
sees and gives light to your body... close your eyes and
relax.....

Close the eyes of your body and open the eyes of your mind
and heart... close the eyes of your heart and your mind... be
aware of the darkness within... Now open the eyes of your
mind and heart and allow them to gaze on your inner being...
and the evening sun that is resting over your whole being.

# 4. Gentleness

Listen to the music and allow your eyelids to rest so your eyes
are focused downwards..... and relax.....

allow this music to awake within you kindliness

begin to look at yourself gently..... lovingly

turn this gentleness towards your thoughts.....
look on them lovingly..... with acceptance.....
allow your thoughts to fade..... and gently smile.

Be aware of your eyes.....their colour..... how you see..... smile
lovingly..... relax

Be aware of your nose..... its shape..... your sense of smell.....
how it takes in the air that gives you life..... smile lovingly .....
relax

Your mouth..... its shape..... the ability to eat..... to nourish

your body ..... the words that you use to communicate .....
pause ..... smile lovingly ..... relax .....
now, in your mind's eye look lovingly at your face.....
allow yourself to relax in acceptance.....
in this meditation you are coming to accept and love 'you'
continue to look lovingly at the rest of your body and the
many different things it enables you to do..... look lovingly.....
smile gently and relax.....
Be aware of your arms..... all they enable you to do.....
to lift..... to carry..... to do the everyday things for yourself.....
to embrace those you love..... look lovingly at your arms.....
allow energy to flow through them..... smile gently and rest .....

Look at your chest and stomach... they carry out the many
activities that enable you to live... look lovingly... smile gently...

Now take your focus to your legs..... their ability to carry
you..... to take you where you wish to go..... look lovingly.....
allow your look to give energy..... your love..... healing .....
gently smile.....

Allow your ankles to relax..... if you can..... calmly move them
in a circular movement..... relax..... look at your ankles.....
your feet..... be aware..... look lovingly..... Rest.....

Feel good about your body..... allow love and energy to flow.....
experience the goodness that awakens as you gently smile at
your body..... experience loving acceptance.....

Listen to the music..... allow love and energy to flow.....
experience a new security about who you are.....

relax..... gently smile inwardly.....

# 5. Emptying

Become aware of the top of your head..... the crown..... like a jug that empties of water, let us gradually begin to empty any tension or discord within us.....
Slowly emptying from the head gradually, gradually experience yourself emptying..... slowly emptying..... down your forehead..... to your eyes..... slowly emptying..... relax..... slowly emptying..... down the side of your face, to your neck and shoulders..... emptying..... relaxing..... slowly emptying..... down your arms..... emptying..... emptying
down to your hands..... your fingertips..... slowly emptying..... from your chest towards your waist..... emptying ..... and relax ..... emptying from your waist to your hips.....emptying..... relax..... experience the emptying down your thighs towards your knees..... slowly emptying..... down your calves..... emptying..... to your ankles ..... through your feet to the tips of your toes..... emptying..... relax..... relax.....
relax in your emptiness.

# Dawn

*Always start meditation with one of the relaxation exercises.*

Become aware..... it is dark.....the early hour of morning.....

you are awake.....

waiting.....for the dawn.....

experience the waiting..... for the darkness to lift.....

and the sun to rise.....

Be aware..... of the darkness.....

you can almost feel it.....

Experience again the waiting .....

Wait in expectation for the dawn..... of a new day.....

In your inner mind..... slowly open your eyes..... to GAZE..... on the sunrise.....

the dawn of a new day.....

Rest in the dawn .....

Feel the dampness of the early morning dew.....

Experience the shadows as they lift.....

..... the faint rays of the warm sunrise on the horizon.....

Rest in this experience.....

Experience the expectation.....

..... the hope.....

..... the recreation.....

..... a fresh start.....

It is the creation of a new day that hasn't been before.....

Rest.....

rest in the hope that is rising within your heart.....

Experience the re-creation of this new day that belongs to you.....

..... own it.....

..... it's yours.....

Allow the sun to rise in your heart..... in your very being.....

The re-creation of your dreams.....

..... unfolding in new hope.....

This is your new day .....

..... Waking in freshness.....

This is your dawn.....

Your hopes..... dreams..... waking afresh under the rising sun.....

Allow the sunrise to touch your hopes.....

Your dreams.....

Allow them to wake.....

..... to be touched.....

To gently unfold.....

..... Remember these are your.....

..... dreams..... your hopes.....

refreshed..... re-created.....

Rest.....

Letting everything go.....

Feel the breeze..... relax.....

Feel refreshed... gaze... rest in the sun... the new day within you

*Scripture: Lk 1:78*

# Door

*Remember to start meditation with one of the awareness exercises.*

I would like you to go through the motion, in your mind, of taking the handle of the door in your hand.....

Now turn the handle..... Open the door.....

If we never open a door
we do not know what lies on the other side.....

Our meditation is journeying inwards.....

To find the door to the centre of our being.....

The storeroom of love..... 'the core'.....

Where life was created in the hands of God.....

It was there at your very centre God saw you..... beautiful.....

..... and loved you..... into life.....

Open the eyes of your heart..... focus on the door.....

Listen carefully.....

Our bodies house our hearts..... our minds.....our souls.....

Our inner selves are bigger than we can ever imagine.....

With our eyes closed.....

Let us start our journey.....

Begin to travel from your eyes..... into your heart.....

Keep travelling..... through your inner being.....

Within you there is a universe.....

Keep journeying inward to the centre.....

Look for the door that opens into the very heart of your being

... Pause.....

... Look at the door .....

When you see the handle reach out .....

Turn the handle... Open the door...

Pause in the doorway...

Gaze at this inner room...

Here lie your secrets...

Your hopes and dreams...

Now enter this room.....

Feel the love... this is the storeroom of love...

This is where you were created.....

Loved into existence...

Experience the energy...

the  courage... the joy...

If there is any hurt in your life... any anger...

now is the time to let it go...

It cannot exist in the presence of love.....
If there is any hurt.....we all have some...
If you are angry ..... have any resentment...

It doesn't belong here .....

Let it go...

You have found 'your centre'...

*Scripture: Lk 11:1; Lk 12:36; Jn 20:19; Rv 3:8; Rv 3:20*

# Now

*Have you started with one of the awareness exercises?*

Immerse yourself in the 'now'

The moment that 'is'.....

We leave everything behind this moment.....

We let go..... try letting  go.....

Imagine you are holding something very heavy.....
you are standing beside a stream, holding a bag..... it's very
heavy..... you can feel it pulling your muscles..... the sinews in
your fingers..... and the pain of its weight is going along your
arm..... under your armpit..... hold on to this bag a little
longer..... in this bag are all the things you don't need for
living..... the anger..... the hurt you carry..... the lack of
forgiveness, the bruises and scars that hinder the 'flow' of your
life.

Anything that stops you loving is rubbish, you find it is
collected and contained in this bag you 'now' hold.

Let it go..... loosen your grip..... open your fingers

'Let go'..... Hear the sound as it drops into the pool of water.....

Watch the pool of water until the bag sinks.

Now you are free.....

Experience this freedom.....the lightness it brings..... 'Be'.

Let us enter the 'now'..... the present.....

Close your eyes and enter into the..... 'now'.....

..... it is timeless.....

Go deeper and deeper into this present moment.............

..... Feel the wholeness.....

Experience the sacredness of this moment.....

The harmony that draws you into the very 'heart of

stillness'.....

Experience the unity of the 'now'..... its fullness.....

..... its vibrant life.............

Allow the 'now' to pull you into this mystery of fullness.....

Each time you draw on the mystery of 'now'.....

or glimpse the present moment....

you find a cup that is full to overflowing.....

'The now'..... is the Cup of Salvation.....that is poured out into

your lap..... and overflowing.....

Rest in the fullness of love.....

Receive his gift......................

*Scripture: Mt 6:25*

# Seashore

*Have you been through one of the awareness exercises?*

Rest your eyes...............

Become still..................

Open the eyes of your heart..............

In your imagination ....

gaze until you see the waves of the sea...............

Listen.............

..... Hear the roar of the waves ................

..... their gentle lapping as they reach the shore...................

..... Stroll along this beach ...

..... Be aware of how you feel ...

..... feel the breeze on your face...

..... the sand between your toes ...

..... Walk closer to the water's edge...

Feel the cold water on your toes ..................

Listen ...............listen to your heart

Hear the rhythm of the waves as they flow to and fro.....

Hear the rhythm of your own life ... to and fro... to and fro ...

Be aware of the harmony of the waves ..... the harmony in your own life..... to and fro..... to and fro ..... listen until you hear the gentle harmony of the waves and the harmony of your life.....

Look out into the far horizon............

As the warm mist covers the skyline.....

Find yourself alone.............

Again experience the greatness of the sea ..............

.............. Hear the lapping of the waves .................

As you stand there small in this greatness ................

..... Be filled with wonder....................

..... In this fullness be aware you are being called .....

..... Follow your call ..............

Allow the wind to touch your being.....

Become transparent............

...................Allow the sea to flow through you..................

..... You are being renewed...................

..... called.....

..... renewed.....

Hear the call?...............

..... Listen..................

Be renewed.....................

*Scripture: Jn 21:1-18*

# Developing World

*Don't forget to do one of the awareness exercises.*

*Before you begin this meditation, take a small piece of bread and share it among the group. Do this in quietness.*

*During this meditation I would like you to focus on the piece of bread you receive, as it is your food for the day..... if by chance you haven't enough bread and there are those who do not receive any, they should focus on and become aware of their empty hands.....*

Begin by being still................................

....................Become..... aware........................

Let this awareness take you to the many different countries in our 'Developing World'...

Assume a first name and become that person.....

..... Where does he or she live?...............

..... Let this become your home..............

Be aware of your surroundings .................

..... How you live......................

..... Your house.....

..... Where you sleep........................

Lack of water..... to wash...........................

..... to drink..................

It's hot..............dry...........................

Does anything grow? ......................

..... Hear somebody call your name.....

What is it like not to have eaten for one day.....

or maybe two or three?.....

Stay with this awareness .............

..... Ponder the way you feel ......................

..... Allow this awareness to touch your heart..................

..... Look at the bread in your hand.....................

..... it's your food for the day......................

..... How does it feel?................................

Now eat your bread..................

..... savour it..... taste it..............

It's your food for the day.................

In the awareness and stillness of this moment.....

Name the country..... The person you allowed touch your

heart .....

Now light a candle of awareness and prayer.
*(One large candle or a night light for each person)*

This candle burns..... burns with your love...............

it carries your prayer..... It reaches out to the  Lord

..... and returns with blessing for those for whom it was lit.....


*Scripture: Mt 25:35*

# Loved

*Always start meditation with one of the awareness exercises.*

RELAX.....

............BE STILL.............

Come into an awareness of yourself................

Allow your body............

your mind............

to be free of thought................

Travel the pathway to your inner self........

Come to your centre..............

..... Rest..............

Grow in awareness...........

Go deeper into the depth of yourself.....

Become aware of a presence......

..... Rest there.....

..... Rest.....

Be aware you are known.....

Come to realise you are where love created you.....

Become aware of the great love that is here................

..... You are loved now............

..... intimately................

You are in the presence of the one who formed you.....

...........................................who held you...............

...............................saw you were good.............

..... loved you into being......................

...................gave his breath..... that you may live ..............

..... Listen ......................... to the song of love ................

............... It is for you ....................

..... You are created in the image..... likeness of God .....

Know you are held in the palm of God's hand .........................

..... You are secure .................

...... looked upon lovingly .....................

Only he knows your inner beauty.............

..... Allow him to reveal it to you ...................

He loves ............ you ................

..... Listen ................

Hear the song of your creation ............

You are conceived in love..... by the heart of God.....

You were born in love by the desire..... and love of God............

................ to give you life ....................

*Scripture: Ps 139; Jr 1:5; Jr 31:3; Mal 1:2; Jn 15:9; Jn 17:26; Jn 17:23*

# Time

*Remember to do one of the awareness exercises.*

Rest your eyes ....................

Allow your body and your mind to become still.....

..... be present to the stillness within you ................

The stillness about you ......................

There is a sense of 'being'................

..... a new depth within....................

Begin to travel inwards .................

Go beyond your thoughts ......................

.............. to the 'centre'..... Discover the seed .....

the seed of time ..................

..... the fullness of time .............. within you ..............

Become aware of 'time' ..................

its fullness ......................

Your life is the earth in which it is sown.....this seed of time .....

Rest in the awareness of 'time' ....................

Ponder over your life ..... holds time ...................

Be with time .....................

..... It calls you into its awareness .................

Ponder over time .........................

................... It holds your life ................

Time is given to you ..................

Become aware of this gift .....

..... 'Be' ............. In the fullness of time .......................

Allow your life to fill this time .......................

..... Time is yours ..................... Own it ...................

Let time take you into your memories .................

Reflect on them .....

Your memories are 'your time' spent.....

Time..... Life.....

..... They are separate ..... yet given to you as one .....

Do not measure your time in minutes or days .....

but by your life.....

..... Whatever you feed the seed of time life gives to you.....

Rest in 'time' ...........................

Time offers you..... the fullness of life ......................

Rest in this fullness.....

Be filled..... The gift of 'time'..... Is the gift of life.....

Given by the hand of love .....................

'Be'........................... 'Filled'.......................

Know time..... its fullness ...................

Its gifts..... It's yours .........................

'Time is'..... You own it ...........................

Know time.....

'Be'..... .In the stillness of time.....................

*Scripture: Ps 104:19; Ps 113:2;*
*Ps 115:18; Ps 69:13; Eccl 3:1; Eccl 3:11*

# Humus

*Always begin your meditation with one of the awareness exercises.*

Come to a gentle stillness.....

Become aware of an inner strength within you.....

Be with this strength.....

Plumb the depth of your inner being.....

Come to know courage.....

Find your gentleness.....

Become aware of what you may think is weakness .....

Look closer within.....

Courage and gentleness lie together.....

Strength and weakness are companions.....

Picture the earth in which the flowers and plants grow.
In your mind walk into a beautiful garden where everything
blossoms, take note of fruit-bearing trees, plants of many
different kinds with their sweet fragrance. Notice the many
different shrubs that add so much colour to the garden. Sit
down on the grass and allow the beauty to saturate your
being.....

Listen to the secret of the garden ..............

Wonder at its beauty....

The 'earth' in which everything grows ..... is its secret .....
The earth takes within it everything that is thrown on it .....
the rubbish..... waste..... often this waste is rotten with the
most foul smell and yet this is what the earth takes into
itself..... and in its digestion turns everything to its good to
produce food for us to eat..... flowers and trees to fill our
world..... thus the earth holds within it weakness and strength,
gentleness and courage.....

Take rest in this garden.....

Savour its fragrance.....

Relax in its beauty.....

Your life is like the earth.....

Experiences of sadness, hurt, rejection,

self-disappointment.....

Anything that has been dumped in your life..... like the earth,

with the weakness with which it was received.....

accept it with strength .....

Turn it to the good with courage.....

In gentleness..... be renewed.....

It is what you do with these that makes your life beautiful.....

These are the things that produce the greatest beauty.....

So again..... relax.....

Rest within your being.....

Slowly repeat the word 'weakness'.....

Experience your weakness.....

Now 'strength'.....

..... Feel strength..... within you .....

.............. experience strength ..................

Courage ..................

..... Realise your courage .....

Courage..... Within you.....

Gentleness..... slowly ............... gentleness ............

Experience its tenderness..... Its peace.....

Whatever troubles you.....

Allow your weakness to reveal it to you.....

Strength to take it.....

Allow courage to turn it to good.....

Gentleness will renew you.....

Close your eyes.....

'Be'

*Scripture: 2 Cor 12:10*

# Spring

*Do an awareness exercise before you begin.*

Relax.....

Come..... find a place within.....

Rest there.....

..... SPRINGTIME IS WITHIN YOU.....

Become aware of springtime..... within.....

Gaze through the meadows of your heart.....

Notice the sun rising in the early morning of your life.....

It overshadows your whole being.....

Notice the dew of sadness.... melt.....

the mists of loneliness evaporate.....

buds of new life begin to open .....

Experience the touch of love.....

Rest.....                    Be.....

with springtime.....

*Scripture: Jn 15: 9-11*

# Precious

*Always start meditation with one of the relaxation exercises.*

Hold something very precious in your hands.....

Marvel at its beauty.....

Be aware.....

Experience the tenderness with which you hold it .....

..... the firmness to give it security.....

the colours that make it unique.....

The more you look ................

the more you are aware of its beauty ..... The more you marvel

Can you imagine if you created this..... so precious.....

so beautiful.....

With what love would you treasure this.....

How much  more precious..... because you had made it .....

Rest in the gaze..... in the beauty .....

............ of something you have created.....

Be aware of your gaze of love .....

Allow it to draw you into itself .............

............. into the realisation that you have been created....

..... You are precious.....

..... held in the hand of love ..............

Marvelled at by God..... because you are his creation

nurtured in tenderness.....

..... held firm in certainty ....................

..... constantly recreated by love ...............

Become aware of this love ..... that is for you .............

Be filled ................

Come to know the love with which..... you are loved.....

*Scripture: Is 43:1; Ps 139*

# If

*Don't forget to do one of the relaxation exercises before you begin your meditation.*

Relax.....

Rest your eyes.....

Journey within the universe of your being.....

beyond your awareness.....

past the passage of feelings.....

to your inner room.....

the centre.....

the still point.....

'Be'

Dwell there.....

This centre is..... love's dwelling place.....

Experience warmth.....

..... the glow that enkindles your heart ...................

Love speaks to you..... Hear.....

He would tell you many things..... if you would listen.....

He will journey with you..... if you allow....................

Yet he will not intrude if you wish.....

He knows the secrets of your heart.....

And will share his with you.....

His gifts are plentiful.....

His love.... beyond measure..... is yours..... if you wish.....

He will accompany you when times are dark ...................

Listen when things get hard .................

help ..... if you ask .....

He will give you warmth in moments of sorrow .....

Offer you joy when things look bleak .....

He will be your light..... in darkness .....

He will be your companion ...............

your friend ..... your love .....

He will not intrude.....

If you wish .........................

*Scripture: Jn 14:14; Jn 16:23; Rv 3:20*

# Trust

**Always start meditation with one of the relaxation exercises.**

Relax ..............

Rest in ..... being ......................

Allow yourself slowly to enter the pathways to your 'centre'.....

Travel beyond your self-knowledge .....

Journey to the mysteries within your subconscious.....

Enter the wonder of your own creation .....

Become aware .....

You are in the hand of your Creator .....

Rest in his love .....

Rest in the centre of 'you' .....

where his love dwells .....

'Jesus' .....          Jesus dwells within you .............

Here he lives ..... he cares .....

he knows you lovingly .....

*Scripture: Jn 15:4; 15:9*

# Look

**Awareness exercises are important, they sharpen your sense and bring you in tune with yourself.**

Relax...............

*We are going to become aware of what it means to..... 'look'..... to 'turn' something over..... hold something in your hand ..... a watch, a ring, even your other hand ..... and look at it as if it were the first time .....*

Be aware of your looking ..... how you focus .....

Come into quietness .....

Rest .....

Begin to centre inwards .....

Become aware of you .............

................ Glance inwards .........

Enter into your inner self ............

Travel past your senses .................

Your feeling ...........

Come to a still point within you ............. rest

Become conscious of something in your life that disturbs you hurts you ............ causes you anger .....

Be with this............

Bring it into focus...............

Hold it in your heart .....

Gently look at it .....

Do not try to understand or reason .....

'Look' .....

With the eyes of your heart turn over .....

Ponder .............

Look .................

Gaze at what you hold ..............

When you look ..... understanding isn't necessary .....

Be ..................

Whatever feelings arise allow them to flow................

Let them go ...............

.................................. Let them go ..............

Come to the awareness of nothing ..................

Be with nothing ...................

Experience..... nothing .....

Experience the .....void ..........

Be with the emptiness .....

Be aware of emptiness within you ...............

Experience emptiness .............. feel the nothingness ..............

the hollowness .....................

Now you are free ...............

Free to be filled..... with the fullness of God ..... (Mary's *Fiat*)

*Scripture: Lk 2:19*

# Moment

*Relaxation exercises quieten the mind and relax the body.*

Rest .....................

Become aware .................

aware of this moment. .....................

Become ...................

................. Enter.............

'this moment'.................

Awaken .................

Draw into ..................

'this moment' .....................

Aware ..... enter ..... awaken ..... 'this moment'

Drawn into this moment ..................

feel the life that is filling this 'moment'.................

the gift ................ of the moment ......................

The nothingness ..... of this moment ..............

In this moment be aware of the giver .................

Ready to fill the nothingness ...............

To create ..... to energise .............. fill .....

Be in this moment ....................

Be

recreated .................

energised .................

filled ....................

*Scripture: Mt 6:34*

# Bereavement

*The awareness exercises are important.*

Relax ...................

Let everything be .................

Let your feelings be .....................

just as they are ........................

Rest your eyes ..... journey into your inner being .....

Be aware of your feelings .....

Pass through the feeling of absolute loss ........................

You are aware of how you feel .....................

The secrets that only two people share ...................

The smile of acceptance ..... that says all is well .................

The touch that says 'You are beautiful to me .....

you are special' .....

The knowledge that you are precious beyond all else .....

The look of knowing .....

The glance .....

Even in a crowd ..... from a distance it gave reassurance .....

The secret of being loved ......................

Of love shared ..............

The wealth of companionship ...........................

The happiness of friendship .................

The joy of being laughed at ..... by one who loves you

The touch of a hand ..... gently reassuring .....
strong in its giving

The laughter .................

The sorrow ...........................

The dreams ........................... fulfilled .................

The conversations ...................

The walks ...........................

Warm nights and long summer evenings..... the gift of love

Your life shared ..... his life shared .................

Your life given..... his life given ...................

Union of love where words cease .................

..... and again life becomes one.....

Endless gifts of love..... with nameless fruits that give us joy.....

Be with these feelings.....

They have made you the person you are .....

Be ......................

Once more travel deeper into the depth of your being .....

to the inner room of your being ....................

to the point of your creation ....................

to 'your centre'.................

Here love lives .........................

This is where your God created you.....

This is where God saw you were very good ........................

This is where he spoke your name and you came to be

Rest in the love of your God ...............

Here God lives among your dreams ...................

He lives among your feelings .................

your memories ....................

your losses.....

..... This is where your God holds 'you'.................

Here at the centre of your being..... you are loved.....

Rest in being loved.....

Be quenched of your thirst.....

Let love renew your strength.....

Let him understand your sorrow.....

Let him temper your pain.....

Allow your God who loves you..... HOLD YOU

For YOU are HIS ............. he made you ..............

He carved you in the palm of his hand..... YOU are HIS

He longs to draw you close ........................

He is in your darkness..... be still ...... Be .....................

Watch for the glow of his light..... his light ..... is his love ........

His love is your strength ....................

Bathe in the light of his love .................

Soak in his strength .................

COME TO KNOW HIS LOVE FOR YOU ...... IN HIM .....

ALL love lives into eternity .....

Experience his love and strength well up within you ..............

He is Your God and he loves you .................

*Scripture: Jr 31:3*

# Reassurance

*Always start meditation with one of the awareness exercises.*

*For this meditation you need a candle, matches and a darkened room.*

Enter a darkened room .....

Be still ...................

Become aware of the darkness .....

..... all you cannot see .....

Be aware of solitude ..............

..... You are a figure alone .....

waiting in the darkness ...............

Be aware of this waiting ................

the hope ..................

the expectation .................

Be..... in the darkness..... listen to the darkness.....

Wait.....

Light the candle.....

Watch.....

The candle slowly lights the room.....

It dispels the darkness gradually.....

Notice.....

the flame.....

the warm glow.....

Be aware.....

Experience a warmth.....

Experience your solitude.....

Light has brought you his presence.....

Allow the light of this flame to draw you into its revelations....

This flame is the Light of Christ.....

The darkened room is your inner self.....without Christ.....

Become aware.....

Of the indwelling of the light of Christ within you.....

Given to you.....by your Father.....

Not one thing had its being but through him.....

All that came to be had life in him.....

A light was the light of all.....

A light that shines in the dark.....

A light that darkness could not overpower.....

*Scripture: Lk 6:12; Jn 1*

# Emptiness

*For this meditation you need a candle and a small bowl that you can hold comfortably in your hand.*

*Begin with some of the relaxation exercises. Light the candle.*

*Awareness exercises are always important to bring you into 'being'.... a tuning in to the harmony that is within..... beyond the conscious business.....*

Sit comfortably..... cup the bowl in your hand ............

Relax ...................

Allow a calmness to flow into you ..............

Experience it ...................

Feel the calmness that warms your physical being .....

Allow your body to warm itself with the calmness that is yours

**Be** .....

Now turn your eyes to the bowl you hold in your hands .....

Gently become aware of its shape.....
..... the hollowness ...................

Be aware of the emptiness.....

.....emptiness..... nothingness ...............

Quietly place the bowl beside the candle ...............

**Relax** .................

Close your eyes .....

Begin your journey into your world within.....

Go through the passage of your hopes and dreams.....

Leave your thoughts ....................

Journey.....

Come into the emptiness within you ..............

.....the hollow...................

.....the nothingness.....

Be aware of the nothingness.....

It is nothing.....

Be with nothing ..................

The hollow ......................
..... the emptiness ..................

..... the nothingness ...........................

..... can be filled ......................

Slowly..... leave this emptiness ...............

Focus on the bowl you placed at the candle ...............

Notice how the bowl is filled with light .....................

Each time you do this meditation and you come to the

nothingness within you.....

to the emptiness................

you will come to enlightenment............

*Scripture: Lk 1:47-48*

# Healing

*Don't forget to start your meditation with an awareness exercise.*

*For this meditation you need a small piece of dead wood, an autumn leaf, or a piece of dead foliage.*

Hold this wood or dead leaf in your hand.....

Gently.....

.....become aware..... of that which you are holding...............

.....Allow to arise within you.....respect..............

**Look........**

............See...........

*Carefully place what you are holding on the floor.*

Rest your eyes.................

.........................Relax.............

Become aware.....

.....Begin to journey the roads to your inner self.....

.................Become aware................

aware ............. What is dead within you?...............

Become conscious of..... what has caused death within you.....

63

..... Travel within............ focus.... Become aware.................

**Tenderly**............bring together what has died within.....

**Look** at it........**Without thought**..............

.......................**Without judgment**.....**Look**............

....................**With respect**....................

The dead leaf... or wood.....is taken back into the earth.....

and gives nourishment to new life.....

Now, consciously take within you..... **everything** that has

died..... (has been hurt)

Place it on the ground of your being .....

Become aware that it is now food .................

**energy for new life**.....

Everything works towards good ..............

**Be aware of death turning into new life** .................

..... **Be**.....                    **Renewed** .....

..... **Life** ..............

*Scripture: Jn 12:24*

# Harmony

*Don't forget to start meditation with one of the awareness exercises.*

Rest your eyes.....

Relax.....

Be aware of a calmness as you begin to relax.....

Allow a peace to flow gradually through your body

Experience this peace.....

In your imagination begin a country walk.....

The day is soft.....

the sun warm.....

the breeze gentle ..............

Feel the warmth of the sun.....the breeze as it brushes by.....

To your left, a large lake..... resting in the sun.....

..... overshadowed by majestic mountains of many colours .....

Notice the lake acknowledge the sun by a gentle reflection of

shimmering gold.....

Breathe in the beauty.....

To your right, the countryside is wild.....

hilly, with overgrown shrubs and bushes of every kind

The many shades of green catch your eye .....

Notice the trees housing the birds and hear their many

different melodies.....

Pause..... stand listening.....

You hear a small stream beneath the shrubbery.....

The sound of trickling water flowing.....

**Be.....**

Listen.....

..... Rustling leaves.....

.............Water.....

..... Bird song .....

**Be** with this majestic beauty.....

.....Breathe deeply.....

Allow yourself to fade .............

..... Become part of the harmony.....

Allow your being to become transparent ................

Everything flows through you.....

touching your being with its beauty ....

In the beauty of this moment..... pause .....

Look into the shrubs................

Notice .... a....small..... perfectly formed..... flower.....

Its tiny head raised to the sun.....

Its colour..... blue..... magnificent in its pastel shade .......

Its perfection stuns you ..............

Its beauty captures you ............

Wonder at its beauty ...........

Continue to walk.....

touched by the majestic beauty of the mountains ..............

the vastness of the peaceful lake reflecting the sun .....

the greatness of this beautiful setting.....

the tiny blue flower haunts you..... in this greatness .....

Small and hidden as it is..... it has touched you.....

In the greatness of its surroundings.... it accepted its smallness

grew in beauty.......................

touched your life ..............

Reflect ...............

Become .............

Discover your own beauty

*Scripture: Mt 6: 25-31*

# Strength

*Always start meditation with one of the awareness exercises.*

Relax................

Rest your eyes..................

.......................................Become aware..................

.............Begin to journey inward..............

Your body holds a world within you..................

A world of emotions..............

..............thoughts .....

.....................feelings.................. ideas..............

The world of your inner being..................

Enter within.....

to a discovery of the unknown..............

an adventure into your universe.............

Become aware of the vastness within..................

Be..... still...................

Open your inner eyes to see the many areas of life...............

the enormous potential within..................

**Focus.....**

Notice the pulse of energy.....................

Sit.............. Be aware..............

Focus...............on your inner energy.....................

This inner energy is yours.......................

Become aware....................

Focus on this energy........................

Realise ................ Your inner source.....

Focus.................. Energy..............

Draw from this source...................

Be filled with energy ...................

**Be.....**

*Scripture: Ps 27:1; Ps 18:1; Ps 18:2; Ps 28:7;*
*Ps 46:1; Ps 59:9; Ps 59:17; Ps 65:6; Ps 96:6; Ps 105:4;*
*Ps 118:14; Ps 138:3; Is 12:2; Is 30:15; Is 40:31; Ps 84:5;*
*Is 49:5; Ep 6:10; 1Co 1:25*

# Adoration

*Awareness exercises quieten the mind and relax the body.*

Rest your eyes ...............

Enter within the sanctuary of your own being .............

Listen .....

Hear the call from within.....

You are special.....

made by your Father.....

called by his Son..... Jesus.....

given..... gifted by the Spirit.....

infused with new life ..................

you were called before time.....

conceived in light..... Jesus.....

held whole in the heart of God.....

..... Enter the sanctuary of your being .....

The ground on which you stand is holy.....

Experience .....

the mystery.....

your creation.....

Allow your heart to be filled with wonder.....

Here God lives in the midst your being.....

Become.....

light.....

..... love.....

goodness.....

Your Father...... The One who brought you into being ......

who conceived you in love.....

.....The creator of the universe.....

who brings all things into harmony.....

has made his home in you.....

**Be.....**

**In the presence of your God..... Be.....**

**Wordless love.....**

**Be.....**

............wonder.................

..... Be ..................

Adore ......................

in Spirit and in truth..... Be ..................

*Scripture: Ex 3:5*

# Evening

*It is good to unwind with some relaxation exercises.*

The day is coming to a close.....

Rest.....

Be at peace with yourself.....

Begin to enter within.....

into the inner universe within you.....

past the business of your day.....

Travel through those many activities that have occupied your

day .....

you are now travelling to the inner sanctuary of your being

past the hassle, maybe anger, joy, hurt, frustration,

the many experiences that have made your day.....

It is time for you to come aside.....

To relax ...................

To 'be' .................

It is that time when the day is drawing towards evening and the sun is setting.

So let us continue to travel inward.

Rest your eyes.

Let us begin to empty ourselves gradually until we come to the 'ground of our being'

the 'centre'

The 'still point' of our turning world.

So again rest your eyes ....

Relax .....

Allow the peace and blessing of evening to settle on you like the evening dew .....

Rest.....

Remain empty.....

Experience the emptiness .....

Relax .....

The evening sun begins to set, casting its shadows of blessing

and warmth over the land of your being, bringing peace and

stillness..... slowly filling your inner being with its warmth.....

The rays of warmth are beginning to fill your life with new colour

Experience this warmth.....

The soft colours that slowly unfold within you.....

There comes a stillness with this evening....

Allow it to envelop you.....

Become warm with gentle new life ..............

Reassured..... with the colours of the Sun......

Become aware that you are at the centre of your being.....

the still point.....

Be aware of the stillness here.....

This is 'you' ............... Listen to your stillness .....

Hear the song of the evening bird in your heart.....

It is the song of your hopes refreshed.....

It is the song of your dreams nourished.....

Listen.....

It is the song of love.....

Love  waits for you each evening.....

longing to bless you.....

longing to heal you .....

Longing to 'be' with you.....

It is your Lord.....

He has made his home in you.....

He waits with love for you to make your home in him....

Jesus waits .....

to bring you to his Father in prayer .....

*Scripture: Mt 14:23; Lk 24:29*

# Appendix: Six-Week Course

This is a six-week course which may be of use to those who wish to introduce meditation within the classroom or as a help to prayer and improved living. These meditations have worked in school and among adult groups very well.

It is good to read any meditation before you give it to a group, so that you can make the meditation your own, with your own emphasis on the script. A meditation is only an awakening of what is already within. Meditation is only a tool, a means to an awakening of the endless potential within each person.

# Meditation – Week 1

1. *A short history of meditation:* The great religions throughout the world practise meditation: Hinduism, Taoism, Buddhism, Judaism, Christianity, Islam.
   In today's modern world large industries, businesses and people in general, practise meditation for stress relief and general good health. One popular method is Transcendental Meditation or TM, and another is Yoga.

2. *Outline talk about meditation.* The requirements for meditation: stillness, silence, awareness, and focus. Meditation is about being present to the 'now'. Meditation is time for 'you', it is one time within the (school) week when you are asked to do 'nothing', not even to think! You are asked to 'be' and enjoy. This time is for you.

- Meditation gives you a sense of well-being. It is the opportunity to take some time 'out' during a busy day.
- It gives you 'time' to get to know yourself better and to realise your gifts and talents.
- It gives you the opportunity to grow in awareness of the goodness and love that dwells at the centre of your being.
- It's a time when you can meet your God.

3. Discuss your own experience of silence or quiet during the day; e.g. Do you do your (home) work with the radio on, or go to sleep to the sound of the radio? When do you experience quietness?

4. *Benefits of meditation:*
- Wholeness and harmony.
- For older people it reduces blood pressure and relieves tension.
- Discovery of your own inner strength, and self-worth, a realisation of potential and gifts previously undiscovered. Meditation, if discovered, is a priceless jewel which will be beneficial throughout your whole life.

5.   In this meditation let us experience the fact that God's love is limitless for **you**, without bounds. And he chose to create **you** because he loves you. God sees you as he created you, **good**, **worthwhile** and **special** to him. The more you come to believe this, the more you will be able to respond to him in love. Meditation that leads you into prayer has untold benefits as it reveals to you the love story of your own creation.

# Meditation

**Adapted from the Prologue of St John's Gospel and St Paul's letter to the Ephesians.**

In the beginning was the Word.....

The Word was Jesus.....

And everything that came to be.....

that was given life.....

..... had life in Jesus.....

You were in the heart of Jesus at the beginning of time.....

You came to 'be'..... had life in Jesus.....

Created by God..... 'in love'.....

..... Given life through Jesus.

When God created you, he saw you were very 'good'.

So let us praise God Our Father.....

The Father of Our Lord Jesus Christ.....

Our Father.....

Who has blessed us in Christ.....

With everything that is good....

with everything that we need for life.....

We are blessed with every blessing of heaven in Christ.....

Before the world was made..... he chose you in Christ

To be whole.....

And holy..... to live in love ............through love.....

In his presence.....................

# Meditation – Week 2

**Part 1.** *Assessment of last week's meditation.*
*A few words on the need for silence.*

The purpose of this time is for you to acquire the tools you need to meditate, and to bring your body and your mind to relax, to enjoy the gift of silence and stillness which, if savoured, will bring great benefits. If you learn the art of meditation it is something that will stay with you, and will give you strength and help you face every situation that life brings your way.
   **Silence is the opportunity for you to take the time to get to know 'YOU'.**
Here is a short story about a stranger you may pass every day, you may say hello, as you pass by because you are rushing to school or hurrying to other activities. You don't have time to get to know the person, but you do recognise him from the outside. As the years go by you continue to say hello, but you never become friends because you haven't spent time getting to know the stranger you meet. To get to know somebody takes time. To get to know 'YOU', you need time, **you need silence to discover your gifts, your dreams, your hopes, and to be happy being 'you'.** If you don't, you will be like the stranger, you will only know yourself from the outside. Today we are going to spend this time discovering the greatest gift God has given to you, which is 'you' .

**Part 2.** Awareness exercises, helping us to be conscious of our own bodies.
   Focusing exercises of the mind as helps to coming to know ourselves in silence.....

**Part 3.** God has given us a great gift, the gift of ourselves – filled with goodness and potential. In this meditation we are becoming aware of ourselves in a new way.

**Ps 46:10-11:** The LORD is with us: Be still, and know that I am God!

**1 Kg 19:11-12:** He said, 'Go out and stand on the mountain before the LORD, for the LORD is about to pass by.' Now there was a great wind, so strong that it was splitting mountains and breaking rocks in pieces before the LORD, but the LORD was not in the wind; and after the wind an earthquake, but the LORD was not in the earthquake; and after the earthquake a fire, but the LORD was not in the fire; and after the fire a sound of sheer silence.

# Meditation

## A reading from the Book of Kings

'Go out and stand on the mountain .....
before the Lord ..... for the Lord is about to pass by.'

For you, is the Lord going to be like the stranger in the story?
Are you going to let him pass by..... what you are doing in
meditation..... is waiting for the Lord.....

Go out and stand on the mountain, before the Lord, for the
Lord is about to pass by. Now there was a great storm, so
strong it was splitting the mountains and breaking the rocks in
pieces before the Lord..... but the Lord was not in the storm,
and after the storm the earthquake..... but the Lord was not in
the earthquake, and after the earthquake a fire..... but the Lord
was not in the fire, and after the fire the sound of sheer
silence..... This is why we are taking time out..... to know the
Lord when he passes by..... He is in the silence..... experience
the silence..... Know your Lord..... I want you to go back to
the word..... 'sound'..... the sound of sheer silence..... Listen.....

Again..... close your eyes..... your body is here..... bring your
thoughts into this moment..... 'now'........ allow the feelings of
your heart to be present here.....

With your eyes still closed..... in your imagination..... stand on
the mountain top..... experience the wind on your face.....
experience the feeling of freedom..... become conscious of the
silence..... the sound of sheer silence ............

'Be still and know that I am God' (Ps 46:10).

# Meditation – Week 3

**Part 1.** In our first week together, you tried to become more aware of how you are loved, how you are held and loved in the heart of God.

Last week I spoke about silence; you tried to experience silence. Just to recap on the quote from the Book of Kings 'the Lord wasn't in the storm, earthquake or fire but in the "sound of sheer silence".' We became more familiar with this 'silence' and with the Lord who is present to us.

This week you are going to bask in the rays of God's love for each one of you in Jesus. To do this you need to become aware of the good that is within you. Each of you has your own talents and gifts, and many qualities of kindness, friendship, understanding, fun and happiness.

Also in the first week, we heard how God has given you everything you need for a good life. Before you start meditation today. I want each one of you to take a couple of minutes to write down what is good and special within you. Once you start to write you'll be surprised. There is so much beauty, so many gifts and talents within each one of you just waiting to be recognised.

**Part 2.** The awareness of your breathing and the rhythm of your own life. Focusing inward with the inner eyes of your mind and heart.

**Part 3.** Continuing awareness of the realisation of God's love revealed through the inner wealth you discover in yourselves.

## Scripture references

**Jr 31:3** I have loved you with an everlasting love.

**Jr 18:6** Just like the clay in the potter's hand, so are you in my hand.

**Is 43:1** I have called you by name, you are mine.

**Is 43:4** You are precious in my sight, and honoured, and I love you.

**Jn 15:9** As the Father has loved me, so I have loved you; abide in my love.

# Meditation

(See exercises p. 9ff)

In your imagination..... hold something very precious in your hands.............

Look at what you are holding.....

Marvel at its beauty..... Become aware.....

Experience the tenderness with which you hold it .....

The firmness to give it security..... the colours that make it unique .....

The more you look.....

the more you are aware of its beauty..... The more you marvel.....

Can you imagine if you created this..... so precious.....

so beautiful.....

With what love you would treasure this.....

How much more precious.....because you had made it .....

Rest in the gaze..... in the beauty .....

............of something you have created ..............

Be aware of your gaze of Love .....

Allow it to draw you into itself .............

..... into the realisation that you have been created ............

..... You are precious..... held in the hand of Love ..............

marvelled at by God..... because you are his creation ..............

Nurtured in tenderness..... held firm in certainty.....

..... Constantly recreated by love ................

Become aware of this love..... that is for you.....

Be filled ............

Come to know the love with which ...........you are loved

# Meditation – Week 4

**Part 1.** Assessment of previous week's meditation.
Awareness of something you feel is negative or anything you might like to change or improve in your life.

**Part 2.** Relaxation and awareness exercises, p. 9ff

**Part 3.** Meditation: Music of the Sea

## Meditation from John 21

This meeting between Jesus and his disciples takes place after his death..... here you find Jesus waiting on the shore, the apostles had been fishing all night and had caught nothing..... Jesus shouts to them from the beach, to throw their nets to the other side of the boat, and to their amazement their nets were filled to capacity..... The disciple Jesus loved said 'It is the Lord'..... Peter immediately jumped out of the boat and ran to Jesus. Then we have Jesus cooking breakfast for his apostles. This all took place in the early hours of the morning. Next we have the conversation that took place between Peter and Jesus. Jesus asks Peter three times 'Do you love me?' And twice Peter replies 'Yes, Lord'. The third time he becomes disturbed and says 'You know, Lord, that I love you' and Jesus says to Peter 'Feed my lambs, feed my sheep', In other words, 'feed my people'.

Close your eyes ............................. Become still.....

Open the eyes of your heart ..............

Gaze until you see the waves of the sea..... Listen .............

..... Hear the roar of the waves ................

..... Their gentle lapping as they reach the shore .....

..... Stroll along this beach..... or sit .....

..... Be aware of how you feel..... Feel the breeze on your face

the sand between your toes.................

If you're walking, walk closer to the water's edge......

Feel the cold water on your toes..... Listen .....

Hear the rhythm of the waves as they flow to and fro.....

Look out into the far horizon.....

as the warm mist covers the skyline.....

Find yourself alone.....

Again experience the greatness of the sea.....

............... Hear the lapping of the waves ................

As you stand there small in this greatness.....

Be filled with wonder.....

Allow the wind to touch your being.....

.................. In this fullness, be aware of a presence.....

Jesus is with 'you'..............

Talk to him ..............

Tell him about 'you'.....

He wants to hear what you have to say.....

He is interested in you..... Feel his love for 'you'.....

Jesus' loves 'you' just as you are....................

Experience his healing.....Experience Jesus loving you...

Once again be aware of the sea

Like Peter, hear Jesus say to you ..... 'Do you love me?'

Answer him ................He replies, 'Feed one another'.....

Again Jesus asks you 'Do you love me?'.....

He replies, 'Love one another'....

Again Jesus asks you 'Do you love me?'

You are being renewed....

called ..........................renewed ...........

# Awareness – Week 5

Awareness is the aim of meditation

Awareness is also the gift of meditation.

Let us discuss the benefits of awareness and what it is.

Awareness means that we are 'tuned in' now, to this moment.

We have discussed how awareness sharpens the mind, enables it to absorb. The hearing 'takes in' what it hears, the eyes register what they see. We learn to function in the 'now', to live and fulfil the present moment. We begin to understand, if we live the 'now', that our energy is not wasted on the past or the future. Life becomes 'full' and 'fulfilled' (Mt 6).

We have been given everything we need at birth, and have been blessed with every gift, but often, through time and neglect, we lose that awareness of what we have. We are now striving for the gift of awareness that we enjoyed in childhood. Let me jog your memory. This awareness is familiar to everyone of us, though you may not have used it since you were very young. Think back to moments when you were much younger than you are now, a small child, when you sat still and listened to the sound of the rain..... or watched snowflakes floating lazily down.

This is the awareness of meditation, without a thought in your head:

Listening ........... gazing..... being .....

Awareness is therefore being awake to the moment, yet free of thought. Meditation is about letting your whole person 'be'.

In 'being', you attain new self-knowledge, and receive a new sense of well-being.

# Meditation – Week 5

In the context of meditation awareness we can understand the words of Jesus in a new way. Listen to his words:

**Mt 18:1**
At that time the disciples came to Jesus and asked, 'Who is the greatest in the kingdom of heaven?'......... He called a child, whom he put among them..... and said, 'Truly I tell you..... unless you change..... and become like children, you will never enter the kingdom of heaven. Whoever becomes like this child..... is the greatest in the kingdom of heaven'.

One of the greatest qualities of a child is awareness.

Is Jesus talking about the awareness that we are striving for now during meditation? Is it the awareness that we had when we were much younger? The awareness that allowed us to 'hear', when we listened, to see when we looked. Close your eyes..... think back to when you were very young..... maybe you sat and listened to the rain beating off the window pane..... or watched the snowflakes..... falling..... feather-like..... individually they fell..... some would melt ..... others would stay for a while..... Remember how you felt... remember the first time you saw a river? Recall the sound ..... the flow of the water..... Did you think?...... Or were you just absorbed ? ..... filled with wonder without thoughts ?.....

**Mt 6:25**
Jesus said to them I tell you, do not worry about your life..... what you will eat or what you will drink..... or about your body, what you will wear. Is not life more than food, and the body more than clothing?

Look at the birds of the air..... they neither sow nor reap nor gather into barns, and yet your heavenly Father feeds them..... Are you not of more value than they?

So do not worry about tomorrow..... Today's trouble is enough for today..... And can any of you by worrying add a single hour to your span of life?............

And why do you worry about clothing?.............. Consider the flowers of the field, how they grow; they neither toil nor spin.

Do not worry about tomorrow..... Today's trouble is enough for today..... Can any of you by worrying add a single hour to your span of life?

Meditation teaches us to live in the present moment ..... to live in the 'now'... Is this not living the words of Jesus?..... it helps us to see more clearly..... if we live in the 'now' this 'moment' each day will be fulfilled.

# Awareness and Focusing – Week 6

You are not asked to talk, You are not asked to think, there is only one thing you are asked to do: be 'aware'.

This time is for you. It is time for you to relax and to enjoy. This is one period in the whole week where you are not asked to think, but to observe your thoughts.

It is said that children smile four hundred times a day, adults fifteen. What does this tell us? Children observe, they are not filled with thinking, they are filled with wonder. As they look they are totally enthralled with the 'now'. Very young children have no concept of 'time', of tomorrow or yesterday. They live in the 'present'. Children know what it is to 'be', hence their ability to smile. They are the perfect example of human 'be'ings. Adults tend to 'do', to feel worthwhile, and maybe should more aptly be called human 'do'ings, often too busy to 'be' human 'be'ings.

I want you too relax..... Allow yourself to be.....

This time is for you..... Enjoy.....

We are going to do the emptying exercise, to empty ourselves completely, so as to leave us free to 'be', to 'observe'.

So relax..... your legs and arms straight.....

Make sure you are comfortable, and relax.....

Imagine a jug filled with water..... watch it slowly emptying..... now allow yourself to empty. Starting at your head, experience the emptying..... Relax... to your head, your neck..... empty..... relax..... gradually to your shoulders, your arms, emptying..... relax..... to your chest, your stomach, ..... gradually emptying .... relax..... to your hips..... your thighs..... gradually emptying..... relax..... to your knees..... to the calves of your legs..... to your feet..... gradually emptying..... relax.

Experience this emptiness..... empty of all thought..... Experience freedom..... freedom to 'be'..... Relax..... empty..... free..... just 'be'..... If thoughts come into your mind, look at them, then allow them to pass through your mind as the clouds pass across the sky..... be empty..... relax..... enjoy 'being'..... Again if thoughts come into your mind, look at them..... and watch them gradually fade into the distance..... Relax..... 'be'.....

It is like focusing a camera. Let us try the same method of focusing. Close your eyes..... remain empty..... what I want you to do is, bring to your conscious mind an experience that has caused you happiness or anger ..... zoom it into perspective so that you can see it clearly, focus, look at it, do not question..... experience it..... and then allow it to fade..... watch it as it fades ..... return to your emptiness..... relax..... be..... (repeat)

Repeat the last exercise as far as 'Look at it..... experience it'. Now allow your experience to take on a colour..... do not think, just be with your picture or experience and allow a colour to emerge, be with the colour, as the colour reveals your feeling, not your thought..... observe the colour..... rest with this..... allow it to fade..... be..... relax..... Still empty..... relaxed..... allow yourself to lie in the sun, it is a beautiful summer's day, feel the warmth of the sun, you cannot look directly at the sun, notice its warm rays as it filters through the branches of a tree, the leaves shimmer silver and gold as they reflect the sun's heat..... relax..... experience the beauty of these moments..... This is God's gift to you, his sun. Bathe in the warmth of his love..... experience the security that love brings..... the reassurance..... Allow this love to warm you..... He is your light..... he is the light of your world..... Do not think ..... remain empty ..... so you may be filled with his love and warmth.

# Posture

It is important that in any posture your back is straight, but not strained. Strain or discomfort is a distraction and does not help either relaxation or meditation. Correct posture helps wakefulness and allows the body to be calm and relaxed. (See posture illustrations, p. 101ff.)

## 1. Floor posture
This position is favoured by many people. It is effort free and comfortable. It helps relaxation and the flow of oxygen throughout the body. It is important for you to lie flat on the floor, your body in a straight line, your arms by your side and a cusion to rest your head.

## 2. Sitting posture (Chair)
It is important that you are comfortable, make sure the chair suits your height, so that your feet rest comfortably on the floor, sit in an upright position, your back should be straight, and your arms resting comfortably on your lap or on the arms of the chair.

## 3. Crossed legged posture
This is an easy version of the Lotus posture. The Lotus posture originates from the eastern tradition, and is beautiful for meditation. Remember that you shoudl be comfortable with this posture, as with any other posture, and that it suits you. You may sit on a cushion to ease the pull of the muscles on your legs. Rest your hands on your knees, palms facing upwards. This position gives a sense of oneness with the earth and enhances harmony.

## 4. Japanese posture

Kneeling on the floor; with your back straight – you then sit or rest on your inner heals. You can, if you wish, slip a cushion between your calfs and thighs. This is the same position for the use of a prayer stool; instead of resting on your inner heals you rest on the prayer stool. The kneeling position is quiet popular and very comfortable.

*1. Floor Posture*

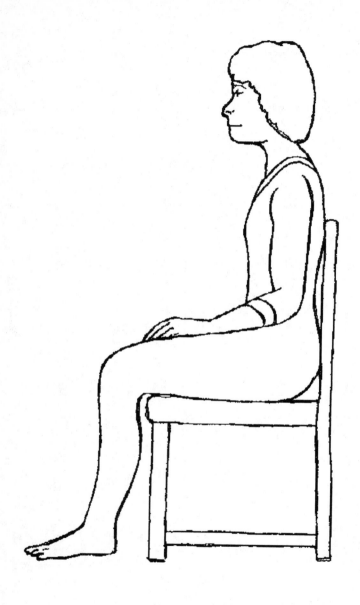

*2. Sitting Posture (Chair)*

*3. Cross-legged Posture*

4. *Japanese Posture*

# Glossary

MEDITATION: puts us into direct contact which means direct experience with who we are in relation to God, the world, others and ourselves.

MEDITATION: is the balance of awareness, concentration, and energy.

MEDITATION: is being.

MEDITATION: is effortless concentration.

AWARENESS: knows what is going on, while it's going on.

MINDFULNESS: awareness of the body; awareness of the feeling; awareness of states of mind; awareness of the contents of the mind.

CENTRE: core, kernel, base, the seat of your being

POISED: calm, composed, peaceful, still.

BEING: awareness of wholeness.

BE: live; is; for example to live in the present moment. Being aware of one wholeness. To 'BE' in meditation is when your body, mind and heart dwell together in harmony in the present moment.

FOCUS: concentrate, to highlight, to centre.

CHRISTIAN MEDITATION: allowing Christ to take

control of our being, leading us to the Father and putting us in touch with the very core of who we are and what we are. Discovering Christ at the centre of our being

# Personal Notes

# Personal Notes

# Personal Notes

# Personal Notes

# Personal Notes

# Personal Notes